Metamorphosis of Zade

by Andia S. Greenlee

Metamorphosis of Zade.

Cover photograph by Ashante K. Greenlee
Back photograph by Andia S. Greenlee

ISBN: 978-0-6151-6966-8

Dedication

To God for giving me the ability to speak
when I did not know I had a voice.

Table of Contents

Introduction

Everyone has a collection, something that displays who they are; and sometimes collections that we cherish can be the window that shows our metamorphosis as human beings. Some build portfolios of newspaper articles, or awards commemorating their child's athletic or scholastic accomplishments while others collect their child's paintings, and occasionally are able to see the stages of a budding artist. For me, it has been my stories, my poetry, and my life on a page.

My first written story was at the age of five called My Cat and I remember being a proud kindergardener as I looked at my first printed piece of literature of about four sentences and four pages long, covered in an arts and craft cover. I continued writing stories and plays, until about sixth grade when I entered my teenage angst at the age of eleven and had an abnormally low amount of respect for who I was, and considered poetry to be a deep and intellectual way of only expressing depressing thoughts. I started out in the basics of poetry, rhyming every line or every other line, until my eighth grade year in middle school when I was taught how to dissect poetry and I discovered other forms of poetry and internal rhyming, which I thought made my poetry sound far less childish (man, was I delusional).

As I look back on each poem that I have written, my first response is to burn them due to how trivial and immature my subject matter was; then I realized it was only evidence of my metamorphosis as a poet as well as becoming a stronger person.

Larvae Stage
of
Poetry

13-16

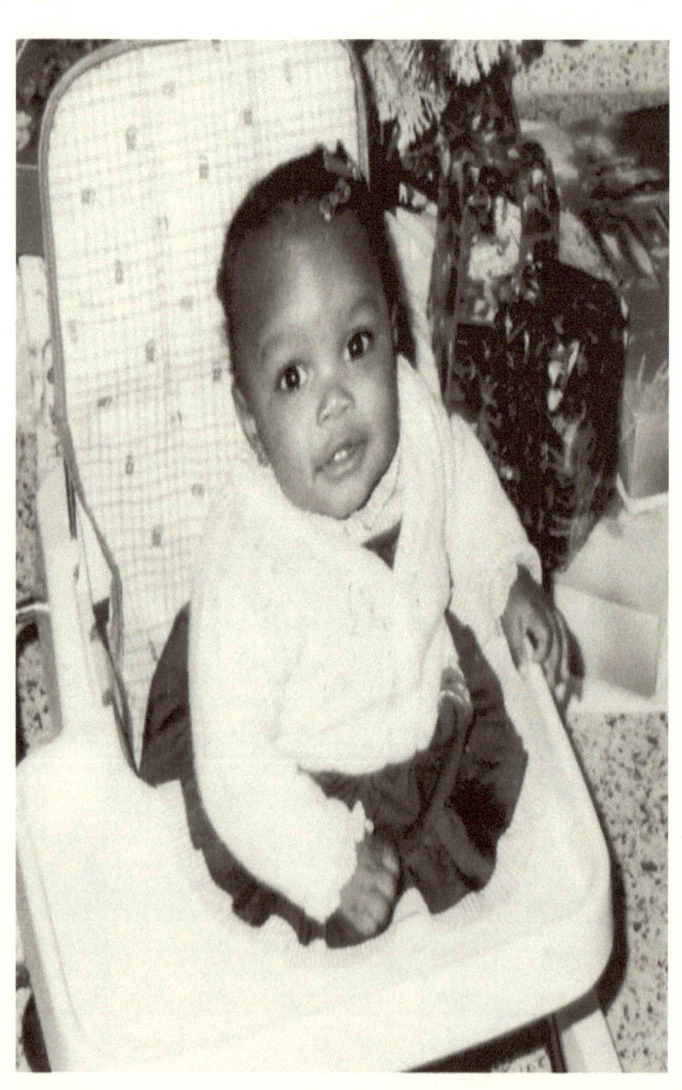

The Library

The young librarian was alone in the
library, a place he called home.
He decided to rid himself of loneliness
by becoming the companion of a book. What
caught his eye? He looked
for the relatively attractive covers, the ones
that screamed his name. He
was drawn to them, but unfortunately the pages between
the lovely temptations were all
just the same. "Not enough substance," he grunted.
"Only a bunch of fluff." But then he heard
a small voice say, "Don't forget me."
He turned to see that the whisper was coming from an
old, tattered book.
"No thanks," said the librarian. "You're not
pleasing to my eye."
"Maybe not to your eye," the book whispered. "But I
can stimulate your mind."

Age 13

Explanation

What is love anyway?
Is it the gifts we bring or
songs we sing to express
our feelings? Someone explain to me

what is beauty anyway?
Is it the way I look, on the
outside? Does it depend on what
color the person is or the size?
Someone explain to me

what is different anyway?
Is it the way I feel, look or act?
Is it the clothes I wear on
my back? Someone explain to me

what am I supposed to be?

Me

A laugh, a cry an unexpected
sigh, the feelings of a lonely girl—me. I'm
bold, I'm shy, and all the while life
passes me by, the feelings of a lonely girl—me. My
heart skips a beat in the presence of a guy, but
they say nothing to me:
the pathetic life of a lonely girl—me.

I cannot let them destroy me. I cannot let them hurt me;
cannot let them know that I am hurt and wounded.

So with a quiver in my lip and my
shoulder with a chip, I hide the feelings of a lonely girl—
me. And
with my chin raised high and staring
straight to the sky, I hide the tears of a lonely girl—me.
Even though I see you with her,
through walls of tears I see you in my future, so
here's a kiss from a lonely girl—me.

Bridge

Two worlds, side by side. She, an
outcast to both, still tries to gain
acceptance.
She came from a dark, unique world, but
it gave her no
affection.
Destiny placed her in that idealistic dimension
between the two worlds of black
and white where all she saw was colorless faces.
Everything was gray, gray, gray.
Each day she built a bridge between the two worlds
hoping that the two would be
like sisters, like brothers,
alike.
Fate thrust her back into the world she came from, but
never belonged to and left her to convince
it of a better life. Instead,
the two worlds collide causing her bridge
to collapse into rubble,
leaving her to pick up the
pieces of a dead dream.

Fraternal Twin

Who is this stranger I
see in the mirror staring back at me?
It is me, plain and nothing to be
vain about.
This person standing in another world, looks
back at me with vanity.
We are one.
She has confidence written on her face. Her body
shows strength and grace. Mystery and beauty
gleam in her eyes. So I ask myself, "Why is
it so hard for others to see my reflection,
and for me to see it too?"

Memory Loss

I don't remember how I felt
when I first began to talk, or when
I took a step toward open
arms when my crawl became a walk.

My mind draws a blank as I sit and
think about whom I invited
to my birthday parties. What flavor
of cake did I have and who pinned
the tail on the donkey?

I can't remember every feeling or
every single place; sometimes I
purposely forget so I can't remember
every face.

I feel so old trying to reminisce about
the past and it is hard sometimes because
the only things I can recall
are the things that happened last.

Age 14

Mirror, Mirror

I asked my looking glass one day, "Who's the fairest?"
and it said, "Beauty on the outside is what
men crave; they do not care to have a body that comes
with a head, nor do they care for her to talk."
"What do they want?" I asked it then.
"They look for girls with a certain walk, and
especially those who give in."
I sighed with dismay
for I was losing hope. I asked, "Is there
a prince that I can find, who
will like me for what's inside?"
"It will be hard, so I hope that you can wait;
what you are asking for
is a species of another kind.
They are out there,
but let me warn you, it shall be
an uncomfortable ride."

Chameleon*

What is that thing that everyone feels,
that urge that no one can describe,
that sensation that makes the carefree hide
that warmth that comes to heal?
It comes and gives life to those who are dead,
but it is also deadly and chokes the heart
and for the weak and naïve, it leaves its mark.
For it comes in many colors, not just scarlet red,
and the infant shoots blindly the golden arrows
while fluttering on wings like a bird.
It comes during the highs of life and it comes in the lows.
What is that thing—have you not heard?
It is a gift sent down from above,
the ever shape shifting gift of love.

*first sonnet

Future Timeline

What will become of me? Only God
can answer that. I'm at a
"bend in the road"
as Montgomery would say—I
can only go forward,
never turn back. I'm living
in the present and that is all I can see, but
I'm curious to see my future,
to see if my life has changed
drastically.
What will become of me? Only God knows
the truth. Will I have fulfilled my dreams and still be living
by the standards I made in my youth? Will I marry,
have kids, or will I still be alone?
No one answers.
All is silent.
Only God knows.

Different

Smiles exchanged but no one
dares to meet her or wants to know what she is about
except
for what societal prejudices feed
them.

Her failed attempt to create an illusion that blends
her in with her lighter peers makes
passer-by's stare, not as if she
were the most beautiful person alive, but as

the black sheep, the ugly
duckling, and all the other metaphorical
children's stories that single
out the odd-looking characters.

Dream Home

Misery has repeatedly blown the straw house
down and Rejection
set fire to the little wooden shack I had.
I called Denial to come and make repairs; I was always
his best customer.

The repairs wore a hole into my pocket, so I invested
in a home with a bit more stability. I
called Bitterness, the mason, and he drew up the perfect
design. There would be

no windows; artificial light
would replace the sunshine. The structure will be strong
enough
to withstand the blows of any storm and
any other harmful disaster I wished to avoid.

I asked him what would be the cost. "Loneliness."
he said. "But you will never
have to suffer a broken heart again.

Speed of Life

First darkness, then light awakens you
and you see upside-down faces, unfamiliar
places. The ground is your enemy when

you fall, but you still want to get up, don't want to crawl,
stepping out of your clear, small, comfortable
box and into a visible one made of steel

and rocks. Who are these people they call
teachers? What is their purpose? Is it to hurt
your head, your fingers, or to dull the lead of your pencil?

Four blank scrolls. Four different lines to stand with
those called peers. Four speeches. Things
called tears. Faces disappear. The flowers

and white dress come into view along with someone's
smile, a band, a kiss. Time stops for a while.
Then in the darkness, something grows within.

Age 15

Inner Enemy

She's crazy like the tornado, breathes
fire like the volcano. Cunning like the
            fox and wise like the owl.
Uncontrolled like a flood, beats hard like the
rain. When turned loose her
            actions are foul.
She is strongest when her dwellings are
free, but it is held by hooks and straps. That
does not make her weak at all.
She is still dangerous, even with weapons restrained,
still capable of destroying her host.
The padded walls do not confine her, for she will find
a way to release her havoc.
She is my mind.

Contradictions

Why does one do the opposite
one feels? Push away those loved and
keep close those hated. "Hated", such a
strong word. More like
"strongly disliked".
Choose always to take for granted the helping hand,
spit in their gracious face,
mercilessly humiliate them,
always begging for their company,
their friendship.
They so willfully accept your pleadings;
you unthinkably repeat the process once again,
failing to realize they actually dare to care for you, only
seeing their sincerity as an ulterior motive.

Ask yourself again, *do they seek to win my affections only*
to seek revenge,
to crush, and
to humiliate me?

You don't know why they continue to associate themselves
with a crazy person.
That's what you are.
Crazy,
crazy in love yet show none.
Funny how one does the opposite
that one feels.

Age 16

She Weeps

Darkness clouds a blazing
red
face.

Gray
thunderhead wraps fingers around remnants of
blue.

World now void of color.

See and feel light trickle,
                    light sprinkle.
Hide away from wetness of gloom.
Dodge raindrops of pain
                    and
                              sorrow
          with an umbrella of
                              materialism
Splash in the
          filthy   sufferings   of
            another.
Dance in it
 without a care of why it rains.
Enjoy it all
          as she weeps.

Hidden Inside a Cocoon

17-19

Remember

Remember,
hide and seek, four squares, duck-duck goose
and the first tooth to come loose?
The time we figure skated with our dolls,
we sent Barbie into a triple axle, but instead she hit
the walls.

Remember
elementary when we learned our ABC's or
the meaning of cruel and unusual punishment when
sitting out at recess
because we didn't obey the rules?
We had pet crickets, beetles, ants and frogs because
Mum and Dad said we weren't
responsible enough to have cats and dogs.

Remember
Crushes on boys and zits on our faces from stressing out
over crushes on boys?
Summer reading lists,
fun so far away (I forget
why we had summer vacation anyway.)

Remember
Basketball games with jammed fingers, bruised knees, and
busted lips?
Skipping homecomings and proms with B.F.F.'s, and
ending some friendships on sour notes.

Remember
administration's concern about our rebellious class and
talks about the "future"
and ten year plans for our lives?
Time has flown, but we've only just begun.
Class of 2002, we have arrived.

Age 17

The Winged Creature

He soars on his horse, Pegasus,
with wings of eagles decorating
his head. He sings a warrior song
with his mighty golden arrows
drawn. His mind is set, his focus
straight, and he charges after his
fleeting prey—me. I run far, far away, but today he is
close. So many times have I met the winged warrior, and
so many times
have I escaped his vengeful claws. Today the hunter is
closer
than ever. His accuracy holds no flaws as he releases the
poisoned dipped arrow and it soars into my cold heart.
I stop breathing for a brief moment. It does not
hurt me at all. The winged creature smiles
and gives the warrior cry as he and
his horse ride back to the sky
and I lay on the ground
feeling warm inside.
The arrow of love
wounded and
killed my
pride.

The Storm

Drowning in it. It's
pounding against my chest. The currents
thrust my heart against the rocks; I am unconscious. My
hcad
bobs for air. I
see you, then I am
pulled under again. The sky is fair, then
gray. I see you
light up and then disappear. I
struggle; I want to be free from this torment. Will no one
help me? I see a hand, I
grab hold, but I am
let loose back into the hungry sea. The hands of the ocean
scoop me up and
roll toward the shore,
throw me on the sand broken and exposed. Now my pain
the world
knows. I
catch my breath, I see you
standing south of me, on the rocks far away. Suddenly, I
realize I am cold and lonely. I
watch the sea
foaming at the mouth and I
dive in once again.

The Day the World Stopped Breathing

Day in and day out, the sun rose and fell on the two giant
brothers, the
Gemini brothers. They were the symbol of pride.
They did not hide but stood boldly for the world to see.
One day before
the sun climbed high,

While the little people below slept or did their morning
duties, there came
a sword from the sky. It was on fire, and its one
desire was to destroy the two brothers. The oldest
awakened first, and as he turned to greet the morning sun,

the burning sword flew and
burst in his heart. The thrower of the sword thought he
had won, but the oldest still stood.
He HAD to overcome. The younger
rushed to aide his brother, but he too soon fell
victim to another sword that stabbed him in the back; the
enemy laughed. There was smoke everywhere,
tears everywhere,
here and there,
falling.

Then, the unthinkable happened.
The unfathomable, unimaginable, impossible happened.

The oldest could hold on no longer, then all the world
heard a loud thunder as the first Gemini
fell to his grave. Then the other waved
farewell as his feet crumbled beneath him.

There were no more Gemini brothers.
They had gone to take their place among the stars.

Then the little people stopped crying.
There was no sound.
All was quiet.

All was still.
There was no noise, for that was the day the world
stopped breathing.

Then the thrower of the swords
threw his hands up in jubilee for it seemed
the battle was over. But out of the cloud of smoke and
debris, the little people
stood high for their beloved Gemini,
for the world to see.

Day in and day out as they pass by
the battleground where the two brothers stood, there is
sadness and they weep like
they should. And they will never
forget that as the two were leaving,
the world, in utter horror and shock, had
stopped breathing,.

Kafka's Leave of Absence

They carry on with their monotonous routines as if I'm
still there with them, but
I'm not there at all. I've taken a leave of absence from the
assembly line to do something
better with my time. There's an ominous void in the
unfinished puzzle,
and when they see the incomplete
picture, they realize I am the
missing piece, but they try to go on
without me, without a second
of mourning. I am left locked in my
unfamiliar room and on my back with six legs squirming in
front of me. I thought this was my
family, but I have no one to help me on to my six feet.
Left to die in misery with an apple
coming from the hard and fleshy exoskeleton of my back.

Age 18

Mountains

Mountains of Jamaica.

Thought the beauty of it all would make me
forget about all the turmoil hidden behind luscious foliage.
The baby orphanage where a boy
would never speak, a girl would never crawl, and
all the other children who were going insane
inside their cages. I still hear unattended cries,
ritual goodbyes. They knew we weren't coming back
to take them. They could see it.

Thought the sandy white beaches would strip me
from the smiles a tennis ball brought to a
dirty face, or that the cool island breeze would blow
away sad memories of that
premature baby
drowning in her own vomit and urine,
choking on her tears, and the fear of knowing she would
not
last through a year.

I thought their motto *Cool Runnings* would be a remedy
to my worrying and nightmares, but
every time I look at those mountains,
I can't forget.

Rejuvenated

Slipping off her shoes,
she wiggled her free toes in the
soft, cool grass.

Released from a
heavy burden
and being comforted by the whispers of
late afternoon breezes.

She never knew letting go of her
hurt and sorrow
could be as easy as taking
off her shoes to let a
tired, calloused *soul*
breathe.

The Ring

Diamond flashes a sparkling smile
from behind the wall of glass,
enticing a pair of eyes. The siren's
hypnotic song brings the hand closer to its
doom as she traps
the naked finger
in her clutches.

Diamond sings of white flowing satin
blanketing the bare wooden post,
carpet of red rose petals and dancing
lace, tissues filled with tears and running mascara,
music and the groom…
does not even exist! None of this exists!
Glassy eyes wake up from cruel enchantments,

Diamond loses her mesmerizing hold, clever Odysseus
broke her singing spell, and eyes and finger
move away from the jagged rocks. Beeswax
drowns out the bewitching siren's pleas and calls to the
deaf
ear, never to be
tricked again into
an empty dream.

Eden

Don't like my bee-stung lips and
my whale-sized hips, but
God saw that it was good.

My backside gets mistaken for a coffee
table all the time, but
God saw that it was good.

I used to get teased about my pineapple
head, and how I had light bulbs
for eyes, and all the while I
wished I was dead, but
God saw that it was good.

Now I don't look at myself with disgust, because
if God gave this body His nod and thumbs up,
I know it *must* be good.

Storyteller

My imagination runs
wild like the violent
Sahara Desert sandstorms. Mirages in the heat
of the ocean desert, I see in
my stories. I become the Persian princess
Scheherazade,
who told
one thousand and one
stories in
one thousand and one
Arabian nights and
one thousand and one
eyes like feathers of a peacock
watch
the storyteller
create her many tales,
which is her life,
to save her life.

The World Through a Black and White TV Screen

It's 10:30 now.
I'm just finishing a class,
have to trudge through the wet grass (can't take
the bus, otherwise
this poem would be
shortened). I
grit my teeth, and walk across
Landis Green.
it isn't green today.
the sky isn't blue,
no white clouds in the sky.
everything is gray.
the weather is expressionless. can't
tell if it's going to
rain or not.
people's faces are deadpan. don't know
if they secretly want to
kill me or not.

a bit cold outside,
my molecules move
slowly
in my body.
as a matter of fact,
everything is moving
slowly.
cars inch
slowly
down Ivy Way because
slow
moving people want to
stay as long as they can in the middle
of the road.
no one wants to move to let
those in a hurry,
pass. They
reluctantly move forward
to let some warmth

through.

by the time I get back to my
room,
the sun has managed to shove a few clouds aside, the
pace picks up, my screen has been upgraded
to Technicolor, and my stomach growls.
It's 11:00.
It's lunchtime.

Rift

Rift stands in the way of two people.
He's not stopping them
from meeting each other half way, but
he is keeping them from crossing him.
They just keep staring at each other,
waiting for the other to make his move,
waiting so they don't have to compromise
their own pride.
One takes a giant leap,
hoping the other will meet him half way.
The other doesn't budge.
He plunges into nothingness
where no forgiveness lies to cushion
his fall.

Age 19

down came the rain

fall into the spun web of no return as tiny spiders
eat away at gray matter,
eat away at that girl's name,
the one you married,
eat away at the unspent time
with your children,
eat away the love you never showed to that boy,
your son.
he needed you, they all did.
where were you?

inanimate objects begin to move,
play hide-and-go-seek
with your mind,
fumbling around in black tar trying to find your
blurry memories,
clouded even when you could see
in the light of day.

down came the rain and
washed the spiders out.

fall into the darkness of the un-lived life as the blanket of
night
eats away at soul,
eats away at that girl's name,
the one you left
your wife for,
eats away at the unspent time
with your children
as they grew up,
eats away at love you never showed to that boy,
your son.
he still needs you, they all still do.
where are you?
can't remember now.

box

plain, stiff, cardboard cube
ignored
everyone passes
no one stops to look inside
even if the inside made them rich

if wrapped in pretty paper
someone stops to take a peek
box is empty
they still admire
the pretty paper on the outside

forgetting they left
empty handed looking inside a
covered box
missing out on something more inside
plain, stiff, cardboard cube

Bay View Window Sestina

A stormy night brought today's gentle breeze
and the blue sky is safe for the birds
to glide. The lovers are welcome on the dock
of Bayview Park; even the single girl
dangles her feet over dancing water
while listening to "Clocks" by Coldplay

and as she played her imaginary keys to Coldplay
she let her feet sway with the rhythm of the breeze
and hover over the shallow water.
Her imagination is interrupted when two love birds
ask her to be their photographer. The girl
smiles as they pose gazing at the sun over the dock.

Her sister is on the other side of the cock
now listening to Coldplay.
The couple is posing for the girl
while their hair is blown by the teasing breeze.
Her sister is feeding candy to the goat-eyed birds
and laughing as they dive into the water.

Seagulls and Herring bob in the sparkling water
and the fishermen on the dock
battle with the catch of the day and hungry, feisty birds.
The sister says the bay looks beautiful when listening to
Coldplay.
Bulrushes are plucked by their musician, Breeze
and the music calms the anxieties of the girl.

Lovers are admired a bit by the lonely girl,
but her jealous eye turns back to the laughing water
and she lets the whispers of the breeze
toss her depressing thoughts off the edge of the dock.
Her sister has finished listening to Coldplay
and now hears the flat notes of crying birds.

The sister runs out of candy to give the birds
and has finished writing in her journal. The girl
sighs as she gives up on her unfinished poem. Coldplay
has finished playing songs and so has the water,
so the sisters decided it was time to leave the dock
and say goodbye to the comforting breeze.

They depart from the cool spray of the water
and drives away from Bayview. The girl
puts her hand out of the window, greeted by her friend,
Breeze.

Unveiling Beauty
20-now

Ingredients for a Love Spell

Childhood spells of love
and matrimony, involving one
single ingredient and a
mild incantation. No frog legs
or locks of virgin hair
needed, just a daisy (or any flower will do)
with petals in numbers of odd. Chant
two phrases again and again, keeping
in sight that sacred name. Bring into light
her yellow face, by pulling off her
pure white veil. Once
her facade is almost bare, pull off
the last piece of her headdress
and utter "he lov,es me". Now, my
child the spell is complete when
when the one you see
comes to thee.

Age 20

Scandalous Rendezvous of the Moon and Sky

Her ebony skin, her
smooth, dark, ebony
skin wears a string of ivory
pearls. She swears
I am mistaken and that they
are really diamonds. Oh, yes
I see the twinkle in them now.
Her ash fur stole floats
effortlessly around her dark, velvety
shoulders. She is dressed for
someone, but not just
anyone. She's not wearing that black, silk dress
for that earth-toned, ruddy looking fellow,
who gravels at her feet.
She is looking at

his ivory face, his
glowing, luminous, ivory
face, which wears a permanent
grin. He swears
I am mistaken and that he
isn't grinning at her, but she
knows he is. They rendezvous every night
but they never say a word, just sip a few
glasses of sparkling dew. They embrace
each other until dawn and then she goes
back to wearing her white collared blue dress
and he scurries away before his
treachery is known.

I know their secret, but I won't tell.

8:20 Curfew

7:15
the bright child, eyes
wide awake of blue, of pale yellow
before bedtime. With
outstretched fingers, embracing my
face and
the earth's face with
a warm kiss of bribery. Earth
returns the entrapment of love with
lullabies to the bright child, eyes
drifting slowly to a green
horizon, lifting lids to see
the movement of people
coming out of hiding to dance
in a blanket of night.
People of tuxedo plumage and
sage green chiffon flutter
under the over-sized protection of
the bird cage, chattering
excitedly, as if there is a secret
waiting to be announced.
7:45
the bright child, eyes
protesting to stay up, protesting
that he isn't tired,
but I see the puffy clouds
of sleep forming around an
orange, itchy eye. The
birds jeer, they know something
is going to happen when
the bright child, eyes
of orange glow, is tucked into
bed. I wait anxiously with
the bright child, eyes
dipping into inevitable slumber. Feeling
something is going to happen when lights dim
and fade, hoping something

will happen, tap me on the shoulder with surprise. I glance
behind my shoulder. Was
it him? No, it was just the breeze, stirring
up the leaves with its soft footsteps.
I wait…I wait…
I grow tired like the bright child, eyes
descending faster, lullabies
taking its toll.
8:00
the bright child, eyes
red from tears, throwing a fit
dragging his feet, lingering
behind trees, hoping to go
undetected. I feel his cold
retraction.
8:20
the bright child, eyes
full of dreams, he is gone,
the darkness leaps out from the east
to begin its dance
and I look to
see what
the anxiety was for. Nothing
no one, just a sunset
alone.

One

Waiting
the entirety of my existence for this
one
moment. Impatiently tapping my foot,
clenched fists
clothed in a ghastly anticipated white.
Waiting,
yet so undeserving of this
one
gift God has made for me. I hold
out hands, which selfishly asked, "When?"
God does not succumb to my whimpers,
nor does He bend to my cries.
Then was not the time
for me to move forward,
to try to step through closed doors.
I beat furiously against them,
self-pity and questions of
whys and *why me*
embracing my being. He
puts a hand up to silence my whine and
points to a door, a lonely door,
one
which God himself opens for me. I am
permitted to go through,
yet I only stand still with hesitation, a
fear of humiliation floods my thoughts. He
gives me a nudge as I cautiously walk in; that
one
step is where we begin together.
Every moment that I am with you
only makes me more thankful for this
one
gift that God made for me; every moment
that I am away from you,
your face,
your touch,
your smile,

only makes my heart grow fonder. And
after what seems like an eternity of
my existence, but has only been
one
day without you, I see you once again,
wrap myself around you and hold
on tight for fear of losing you,
for fear of going another day without you,
for fear of becoming
one
once again and completely without you. I
Close my eyes, exhale a silent
thank you to God for my blessing of
one.

Color Me Love

A cage, white dove fluttering
inside a brown box labeled "FRAGILE. THIS
SIDE UP" Hear the rapid thumping of a
bloody muscle pumping red oxygen
to the gray matter upstairs in the
attic. Listen to the
shattered pieces,
one thousand and one
pieces, jingling, jangling within the package,
shaken not stirred.
Watch as it all turns to blue soma spilling
on the floor and you muttering
to yourself, "What a mess I've made again."

See the spider weave her beaded tapestry
of dew and web, the curious cat entangled in
a ball of yarn, and a pair of impossibly knotted
shoelaces, ensuring no possible escape.
Strategically place your right hand on the red dot,
your left foot on the yellow dot,
twisted among other bodies. Avoid falling
on your face again.

The amber glow of a cozy fire in the
dead of winter,
the sizzling pavement on the
Fourth of July, and that
drive to get the promotion and the bonus--
within the same month.

Hear the sound of that pink laughter of
babies that gives birth to fairies
in Neverland, the whizzing of golden arrows or
the black, lead arrows carried
by the mischievous hands of a winged infant,
the hand prints left by the sun as
it plays Saturday morning tag with the green leaves,
and the smile of a Father as

He watches His baby girl take her
first steps into womanhood.

Love is that white peace, that
fragile blue. Love is the
gray area of knotted confusion and
that passion fruit
red. Love is that mystic pink of innocence and
beauty's green. Love is color.
Love is God.

Age 21

Skin

Pulling at it, making sure it all fits
snug, tight.
Born with it, but I never wore it right
by the world's view. There's more to me
than brown skin gleaming in the sun,
but feel free to pinch me;
wake me up from dreaming about being
someone else.
It sags toward the earth instead of snapping back.
Stretched
to fit a mold of
assimilating into popular culture, being "black", or
being me, a mixture of it all.
Stretched.
Everyday I am stretched, instead of growing
in the mold of my Creator's hand.
Stretch marks form; I count them, there are twenty-one,
in April twenty-two.
Hanging loosely on fragile bones
like an overcoat instead of that cute
leather trench coat I saw on that girl yesterday, I stare
at a Picasso painting, struggling to regain
my identity,
my face,

me.

VCR

rewind.

opening the front door, saying
goodnight to rowdy boys
in the living room, shuffling backwards upstairs,
replacing faux contentment with
soggy, salt stained cheeks.

opening the room door, my back facing you, then
turning around, saying goodbye as I hug you
in the silence of muffled sniffles and hot
teardrops rolling upward, back into my eyes.

opening the bathroom door, saying
what did I do wrong? wallowing echoes
bounce off hollow walls, as I place once crumpled
tissue back on the roll smoothly, unused. I look
into the mirror, and my blood shot eyes begin
to clear up.

sitting on the bed, as a bewildered stare
turns to timid smiles and nods.
what are you trying to say? listening
ever so intently as you pause
between thoughts. There is a silence.
I stand up; you
pat the bed, cue for
me to sit down.

record.

boy: man

the other night,
I saw a broken boy
age one behind a score.
eyes full of shame that
splattered on his
humbly bent knee.

I saw a broken heart
encrusted with guilt
age one behind a score.
soul submerged in past failure that
choked out his life,
his identity.

I saw a broken life
that I was a part of and
responsible for
it being in this broken
state—asking to be forgiven,
asking to be transformed.

I failed him.
I failed myself.
I failed God.

the other night,
I saw a broken man
age one behind a score.

Beyond Mr. Roger's Neighborhood and the Land of Make Believe

Go to a place of familiar nothings
and lose your shadowed past. A
place where happy dreams can give a person
wings to fly, and imagination is key
to your survival. Moments lived float
effortlessly through your mind until
the only memories remembered
are the ones not left behind.
Say hello to that familiar stranger and
feel you have known him for years.
Upon arrival to this new place past the stars and
on till morning
you realize you never left home.

Go to a place past the burning lantern
and find that your deepest fear
becomes your greatest strength. The roar
of a lion brings comfort and peace
and holds all the magic in the world. You cannot
reenter the same way you came and
seeing is not believing, only a lack of faith.
Your past becomes your present, your
present becomes your past; you never miss a beat
with either, whether you jump forward or
jump back. Even Father Time is
allotted a moment to lay in slumber

for the days of this world and yours are
numbered with precision. The end is
inevitable, the path through your closet is
closed forever, and the pearls wrapped 'round
your neck become the gate
which separates the mortal man from the immortal, Hook
from Peter Pan, and Time from Eternity;
but you may climb
higher, Higher, HIGHER still.

Alabaster Jar

I knew of a woman,

who walked
down a lonely road. Sold her body
to the world, its love she had never
known. It used and abused her
heart is numbed by nova cane. Each night
as she sleeps she cries, "Love, please
come my way."

I knew of a woman,

who lived
on the corner. She was a walking ad for
man's guilty pleasure. Each coin that she earned
she used to buy her life some worth, but the
jar, which contained perfume, only
made her despise her birth.

I knew of a woman,

who walked passed the
Pharisees, who only saw her for what she
was and not all that she could be; but there
was a man who knew, she was worth so much
more. As she looked in his eyes, she said,
"This is my open door."

I knew of woman

who fell down on her knees and cried,
"Dear, Jesus please relieve me of my
misery. Can you remove my shame, my pain,
and suffering? Make me whole
and erase my iniquities. I break my alabaster jar
full of sin and pour it on your skin, God make me
whole again."

I knew of man

who walked down a lonely road. Gave
His body for this world, His love He had
always shown. We use and abuse Him, our
hearts turn from Him every day. As He
hung on the tree, He cried, "I still
love you anyway."

E37 Current

awaken me
from my slumber amongst
the dry bones
of a national graveyard.

stir within me
a fiery passion, which consumes
death around me and
cannot be quenched.

give me
my wings to migrate
to your calling, a voice only
few will hear.

let me
drink of a spring that
turns my soul into
a rushing river.

fill me
with your warm
breath of life and power
to say to the grave
“rise up and LIVE.”

LIFE

let us
make a silent noise
for those who cannot speak
out and voice their cry.

let us
make a silent scream
for those who taste death
before breathing life.

let us
cover our speech with a one word,
red strip that is
more audible than the sound of our voice.

let us
cover our lips with a
red, atoning blood that saves and gives
the unborn dream a choice

to live or die, to walk in His plan and
accept their divine appointment
to pray for a nation, which is

numb to God's purpose and
creating a generation of
the walking dead.

it's time to inhale the fire, and exhale
the ash. Breathe in the water,
and breathe out the trash and replace it
with **LIFE** sticking close to your
lips, utter that silent sound
to heaven, and stretch out your hand

to a people who are blinded by a darkness,
to a people unborn, to a people
aborted by a lie.

Solitary Confinement

my body rejects food;
only craving the sound of? Your voice
satiates my hunger.

during those times of starvation
am I raptured into a disillusionment or could I
really be entering into Your reality?

my spirit is agoraphobic;
only the company of solitude brings me into Your
city of angels.

during those times of loneliness
have I created a ghostly friend to talk to or could I
really be conversing with my Father?

my heart is humbled;
only the bend of my knees and bow of my head could
move a King to grace.

during those times of poverty
did I wallow in my sorrow or did I humbly beg
to be forgiven?

Angry Cup of Black Coffee

Coffee
served black.
Out comes my pink
tongue of disgust, repelling
that domineering, tough
leather taste on my lips. So
bitter is the

Coffee
served black.
Boiling feverishly over the
exploitation of its ancestors,
the coffee beans, and
repulsed by the idea of
mingling with
pure white sugar and
silky French vanilla cream.
They are waiting to civilize the untamed

Coffee
served black,
replacing its taste with its
lighter counterparts:
the romantically melting Italian cappuccino or
the soothing Celtic Irish crème—
making it lighter, more acceptable to
my taste buds, ridding it of its
barbarous darkness.

I like my coffee how I
like my men.

I Am Not

Black, I am not,
though darkness shadows my skin.
"Black" does not define me.

Colored, I am not,
though the hues I reflect suggest otherwise.
"Colored" does not describe me.

African, I am not,
though ancestors traveled across angry seas.
"African" does not characterize me.

What does categorize me?

Woman I am, not
a color picked out of a crayon box.
Strong I am, not
meant to be enslaved by the past.
Instrument of God I am, not
an object used for some political agenda.
Andia I am, not
a box I check to fill your quota; but
if I must check one, I

check *Other*_________.

Age 22

Rift (Part 2)

Stuffed inside the belly of Rift, hostility
and despondency stretch him wide,
until reconciliation seems
impossible for two people to achieve. But
animosity's flame
wanes over time, and where love
once ebbed, its high tide now flows gently through the
gorge to bury all past
transgressions. A bridge is built, one of forgiveness
and humility—not by
one, but two people, who are willing to close
Rift's gaping mouth in order to
mend a broken friendship.

Donahue

Little girl, little girl,
with eyes of paradise blue and
skin so toasty brown
from spending your days in the sun,
        why are you crying?
Despite the radiance of your gap-toothed smile and
freckle splattered face, I see
the heaviness that draws you back from experiencing a
happy place you only pretend to know.

Little girl, little girl
with eyes a tropical hue that
entice me to wade in a little farther until
I am sinking into your internal sorrow,
        what are you hiding?
You will let the sun kiss your skin, adorned
in poison ivy and mosquito bites, but will not let warm
fingertips brush past
the deepest part of your soul.

Little girl, little girl,
with eyes a stormy azure and
skin bleeding from scratching at life's rashes
and picking at its bites and scabs,
        do you know you're slowly dying?
You cling on to a deadly comfort that has
vaporized thirteen years of your life, leaving
you to peel back the burnt skin, and abandoning you
with no emotion except an apathy for living.

Dancer

I hold my rigid pose as I
wait for the music of my life to play. Spotlight
delicately traces the hard edges of my
body, and synthetically warms my back. The lonely
beat
calls to me from my translucent, woven basket and I
answer it with a serpent's sway,
side to side. A step forward with my left,
back in place,
a step backward with my right,
back in place. I dance for no one, but for that artificial
light, hanging above in metal rafters, and for the silent
darkness, whose eyes are ever fixed on me. I glide across
the stage, the spotlight follows; I spin
in place, the spotlight follows me with a pleasing eye.

I make my mark on this stage with my body
PUNC-tuating
every drum beat.
My hips
bang, bang
and leave no room for
Bitterness to lead
my dance; my outline becomes softer.
My feet
stomp, stomp
on the toes of Rejection, until he feels the pain I feel
when I let him guide my steps.
I do not need an audience; I do not need
a leader for my own dance. I excel
with the beat, spinning
round and round,
flinging my heavy thoughts from the
hem of my skirt. The beat is
going, going,
my lungs heaving
up, down, up, down,

until the music stops.
The spotlight grows cold, and I
fall to my knees as the darkness I tried to release from my
being, floods my soul; I
was foolish enough to think I could easily lose it like a
shadow, but
I am shackled once again.

Leader

Another spotlight—not from above
in the rafters, but from within another Dancer—
ENTER STAGE RIGHT. His radiant presence
swathes the whole stage and
reveals a shackled me. I am loosened
by one gentle touch of His hand; He welcomes my hand
into His as a different song—one that seems
to be coming from Him—begins to dictate
our movement. He steps forward,
I go backward; He
steps backward and
pulls me forward.
He spins me, then
snaps me back into a serene,
rhythmic embrace. The spotlight He shines
peels the darkness
away from my dry and flaky soul
like a banana's skin, revealing a pair of wings, cocooned
by my anguish.
He lifts me above His head as if I had carried no more
weight of my insecurities; He carries them now
and I am free, my dance is complete.
He lowers me and as my feet kiss the stage, the darkened
audience awakens and applauds—
not for me, but for the Dancer
who shines through me.

www.ingramcontent.com/pod-product-compliance
Lightning Source LLC
LaVergne TN
LVHW050941080826
845145LV00004B/1361

* 9 7 8 0 6 1 5 1 6 9 6 6 8 *